When You Have Doubts

When You Have Doubts

A Book of Comfort

Alvin N. Rogness

Augsburg
MINNEAPOLIS

WHEN YOU HAVE DOUBTS
A Book of Comfort
by Alvin N. Rogness

1999 Augsburg Books Edition.

Text of this edition originally appeared in *Book of Comfort,* Copyright © 1979 Augsburg Publishing House.

Cover design by Craig Claeys; interior design by Michelle L. Norstad.

Acknowledgments
Scripture quotations are from the New Revised Standard Version © 1989 by the Division of Christian Education of the National Council of the Churches of Christ in the United States of America. Used by permission.

Library of Congress Cataloging-in-Publication Data

Rogness, Alvin N., 1906-
    When you have doubts : a book of comfort / by Alvin N. Rogness. —
Augsburg Books ed.
        p. cm.
        Includes bibliographical references.
        ISBN 0-8066-3840-0 (alk. paper)
        1. Faith. 2. Consolation. 3. Christian life—Lutheran authors.
I. Title.
BV4637.R625 1999
248.8'6—dc21   98-49366
                                                              CIP

Manufactured in the U.S.A.   AF 9-3840

03   02   01   00   99   1   2   3   4   5   6   7   8   9   10

Contents

Preface

You and I are on a road of sharp turns and sudden dips. And there's fog, thick fog. Sometimes boulders block the way. We neglect the map and are lured into detours. Weary, we may want to give up. We cry for comfort.

There is comfort. Years ago God said,

> Comfort, comfort my people. . . .
> Speak tenderly to Jerusalem, and proclaim to her
> that her hard service has been completed,
> that her sin has been paid for,
> that she has received from the Lord's hand
> double for all her sins.

God yearns to comfort us—but on God's terms and in God's way. If I call on God, I understand that he may have to stop me in my tracks and turn me around before he can be gentle. God may have to use the scalpel before he can heal my pain.

In these short chapters I've tried to describe stretches along the road. I've traveled many of them. I'm old enough to have learned a little about them. But I'm no heroic traveler. Many times I've rejected God's comfort and tried to go it alone. Often I've been puzzled about the kind of comfort God seemed to give.

I have the map, the Word of God, God's wisdom and promises. And I have a Friend who has walked the way before me and who walks with me now. His hand is on me to lead me and to hold me. There is no greater comfort than that.

1

When Doubts Torment You

You doubt that which you most want to believe. Your child is very sick. The doctor says she'll get well, but you worry. What if the doctor is wrong? Doubts keep welling up, and they don't subside until your child is back home, safe and sound. A man may have no reason to doubt that his sweetheart loves him, but he may worry about it, simply because losing her love would shatter his life. You doubt that which you most want to believe.

No one doubts that which can easily be proven, such as four plus four equals eight, or Napoleon once ruled France, or the Missouri River flows into the Mississippi River.

It's in the field of religious beliefs that doubts are most harassing, because faith in God is ultimately the basis for faith in almost anything else—other people, the future, even oneself. If there is no God, what is there to count on? People don't worry much about whether there is a God until they very much want a God. They don't bother with whether Jesus is the Son of God who forgives sins unless they feel the burden of guilt and sin.

In the New Testament we meet the apostle Thomas, often dubbed "the doubter." Jesus appeared to the other disciples after the resurrection, but Thomas was absent. Told that they had seen Jesus, Thomas in anguish said he could not believe unless he could touch Jesus' hands and side. He doubted, precisely because he wanted more than anything else to have the Lord be alive.

When Jesus did show up to Thomas, he chided him, "Because you have seen me, you have believed; blessed are those who have not seen and yet have believed." That's you and me, and the whole human race, ever since the Lord's ascension. Like Thomas, we may be plagued by doubts. Given no vision in the sky, we are summoned still to believe. And deep down, we want to believe.

A philosopher has said, "The promise is so vast that a feeling of incredulity will creep in." And what a promise the biblical story holds! Back away from it for a moment, and look at it as for the first time.

We say that the God who created and manages this vast universe decided to colonize a tiny island, earth, with his family, his sons and daughters. And, that when his children turned from him and were imprisoned by the enemy, instead of abandoning them, God came to earth in the person of Jesus, God the Son, to win them back—at the fantastic price of giving his life on a cross. We go on to say that this God gives each of us an open line to him. We can dial God direct, and the line is never busy. God hears our most trivial prayer. And when death is done with us, God puts us on our feet again in a more wonderful part of his empire to live with him forever.

Is there any other story in all the world to so tax our imaginations? How can modest people believe they are important to God? Doubt seems more reasonable—and humble—than faith.

But to doubt leaves us on an uncharted sea without a rudder. If the story is not true, then what? What is my importance in this universe if I'm not a child of God but merely a blob of protoplasm? Is the universe itself any more than a cold, impersonal, and cruel machine, if there is no God? Is there any reason to struggle for justice and mercy and righteousness?

The option of doubt is really too frightening to entertain. An empty heaven, no judge on the bench, no Savior to forgive, no good Father waiting for us. In *Pippa Passes,* Browning says, "This Christianity, it may be so or it may not be so, but will you have it be so if it can?" We answer that, more than anything else in all the world we want it to be so, all doubts notwithstanding.

Faith is stronger than doubt, because it attaches itself to the truth. Doubt is wedded to an ultimate lie. And God had other ways than a laboratory or a computer to give us his own kind of "proof." We are not left to wishful thinking alone. We do not create God in our image. We are created in his, and he has provided us with built-in connections to him. "Deep calls to deep," says the psalmist. And Paul says that God's Spirit witnesses with our spirit that we are God's children. There is a profound intuition in the human spirit that will not settle for a harsh, impersonal, and indifferent universe.

Robert Ingersoll, a late nineteenth-century agnostic, said at his brother's grave:

> Life is but a narrow vale between the cold and barren peaks of two eternities. We strive in vain to look

beyond the heights. We cry aloud and the only answer is the echo of our wailing cry. From the voiceless lips of the unreplying dead there comes no word, but in the night of death hope sees a star, and listening love can hear the rustle of a wing.

We have more than an echo. God has broken the silence. God has spoken to us through the prophets. He has appeared in the person of God the Son. God's Spirit broods over us through Word and sacrament. And through the centuries God has provided a cradle of believing people, the church, in which doubts lose their hold, and we are caught up in a kingdom, at once mysterious and real, where we find the key to life.

We live by faith, not by sight.
  2 Corinthians 5:7

2

When You Feel You Have Lost God

Read the Bible from cover to cover, and you won't find God asking you to feel one thing or another. God has much to say about what you do, but not about how you feel. You may have lost God, but not because you feel you have.

Feelings are capricious. You have little control over them. You do have something to say about what you will to do and about what you will to believe. But even when you believe the truth and do the good, you still may feel down. Don't worry about it.

A lot of fine people have been sent reeling down an unhappy road because someone told them that they ought to feel something to find favor with God. Someone asks, "Haven't you had the feeling that God is near?" or "When did you first feel that God had forgiven your sins?" or

"When did you first feel that you loved all people?" or "When did you really feel that you had come to Christ?" Implied in each of these questions is that at some high point you should have had an overwhelming feeling about God. And maybe you haven't had it.

I like what Jesus told his followers: "If any one chose to do God's will, he will find out whether my teaching comes from God or whether I speak on my own." If you are to know and to feel, you'll have to experiment by doing his will. In no way can you sit back and meditate or study and hope either to know the truth about God or to feel anything about God. You have to plunge into doing God's will, despite all your doubts and all your uneasy feelings.

We can't dictate to God what kind of feelings he should give us. And there's something very sad about people who run from one church to another, hoping to get some kind of feeling. If they think they have found the right feeling with one group, often they reject Christian brothers and sisters—even family members—in another group.

God gives assurance in his own time and in his own way. God gives feelings too, but we can't dictate what kind of feelings he should give us. God's test is neither in assurance nor in feelings. Jesus made that clear when he said,

"Whoever does the will of God is my brother, and sister, and mother."

Unfortunately, in our day we have concentrated on feelings, often in a disastrous way. A moving picture marquee had the slogan, "If it feels good, it's OK." What nonsense. If it feels good to murder, it's OK. If it feels good to commit adultery, it's OK. If it feels good to get another spouse, it's OK.

You can't trust your feelings, even about God. For nearly two thousand years the people who have taken Christ seriously have had something to tell you about God and the Bible. You had better trust them instead of your feelings. If you don't, you'll be on a roller coaster, up and down, and you'll have no comfort at all.

Go back to the wonderful message of the Bible. It tells you that God created you, redeemed you, and claims you as his own, no matter what you think or how you feel. Fasten yourself to that promise, and don't let it go. God will give you the feelings you may need. Do God's will, as you discover it, and let your feelings fall where they may.

God has said, "Never will I leave you; never will I forsake you."
Hebrews 13:5

3

When You Don't Feel Religious

I get a bit puzzled, and disturbed, when my friend says, "I'm not a religious man." What does he mean? Most likely he measures himself by the absence of some sort of feeling he thinks he ought to have. He may believe in God and in Jesus Christ, and he may be a person of integrity and charity, but he thinks he doesn't feel religious enough to be a Christian.

Nor is his situation made easier by the current fashion of people telling others about the high moment when they became Christian, even implying that they've since been riding some cloud of untroubled peace and joy. So my friend goes his troubled way, thinking that if he can't match the emotional ecstasy of well-publicized born-again people, he's outside of the family of God.

I admit that I have mixed feelings when someone "witnesses" to some remarkable experience he's had with God. On one hand, I am encouraged by his new enthusiasm and ardor, and a bit envious. On the other hand, I'm haunted by the uneasy feeling that, to be a full-fledged Christian, I ought to be able to match his ardor, and usually I can't. So should I run around looking for some experience?

I take encouragement from the apostle Paul. Who can match his experience on the Damascus road? He was struck blind by a blazing light. He heard the voice of Jesus. But he hardly ever mentions this to anyone. In the New Testament record, he refers to this remarkable moment only twice. Even then, he talks about it in guarded language: "God was pleased to reveal his Son to me, in order that I might preach him among the Gentiles."

Paul must have known that if he dwelt on his particular experience, he might mislead people into thinking that they would have to have a similar experience if they were to be followers of Jesus.

Don't get me wrong. A life with God will generate feelings far more profoundly than a symphony or sunset or the words of a loved one. But our Lord was far more concerned about moving the wills of people than moving their feelings.

If you help your grumbling neighbor when you don't feel like doing it at all, if you are patient and uncomplaining when you feel like blowing your stack, if you come to church to thank God when you feel depressed and dejected—in short, when you defy your feelings and do what you think is right—you're probably much more "religious" than if you were to wait for some celestial feeling to overcome you and sweep you into action. We have little control over our feelings. We have more control over our wills.

Moreover, how do you measure the intensity of a feeling? Let us say that two men fall in love with two women. One man is exuberant. He tells everyone about his love. The other is restrained. He tells no one. He has trouble telling even her. Are we to conclude that the noisier one has the deeper feelings and will be the more devoted husband?

My mother was quiet and humble. I doubt that I've known anyone more devout. She always felt a bit uncomfortable in the "witnessing" groups, and I think she lived with some uneasiness that she couldn't be loquacious about her Lord. But it wasn't necessary for her to expose her feelings for us. We knew how deep they were. Her life was an eloquent revelation. In spite of this, she may have gone to her grave wondering if she was "religious" enough.

Most people who have a striking spiritual experience will face two dangers. First, they may always refer back to this one instance for validation, and forget about the hard, sometimes uninspiring life of the disciple. Second, they may leave their Lord altogether if they fail to experience repeated high moments. They forget that they have no right to dictate to the Lord what feelings he should give them.

I remember a wonderful, devout woman dying from cancer. Two days before her death, her daughters came to me and told me their mother was in deep distress because she didn't think she was good enough to have God accept her, though they had assured her that she was the best of mothers. I went to see her. She poured out her heart to me. She said, "Not only am I not good enough, but I have deceived my daughters into thinking I'm better than I am." It didn't take her long to remember that her status with God depended neither on how well she had done nor how dedicated she felt, but on the simple, great truth that Jesus Christ had died to make up for all her failings, both in doing and in feeling.

If you are among those who say, "I'm not religious," please take stock of what criteria you're using. Are you depending on your feelings to qualify you? Are you under the impression that your life must be faultless before you can approach God? In either instance, don't read yourself out of God's family.

You have a right to come to God in boldness. Rely on God's promises, that he receives you as you are (because Christ has opened the door for you), and push on into the kingdom to claim the comforts and joys and duties that await you.

> *Now faith is being sure of what we hope for and certain of*
> *what we do not see.*
> *Hebrews 11:1*

4

When the Bible Puzzles You

There's no book in all the world's literature that has so profoundly shaped our lives as the Bible. It's not one book, really. It's a library of sixty-six books, some perhaps 5000 years old. Not until a.d. 400 were the last books, the New Testament's twenty-seven manuscripts, accepted into one collection.

We call it God's book, the Word of God. Obviously it was not published in heaven and dropped down by angels. It is a record of what has transpired in the lives of people who took God seriously. Through its many literary forms—history, parable, drama, poetry—we believe that God reveals himself to us and comes to us.

It has not been easy to escape two extremes in dealing with the Bible—on one hand, to think of it as virtually having dropped down from heaven, with every word and comma in perfect order, and on the other hand, to put it in the same class with all great, inspirational literature. Neither extreme satisfies the believer.

To regard the Bible as perfect, correct even in all its historical and scientific allusions, puts the believer on an endless chase to defend it against historical and scientific research. To think of it as just another great book among others is to rob us of its divine revelation and authority.

Even if we want to regard the Bible as perfect, we do not go to it to learn about the shape of the earth (Christians did this in the day of Galileo and Copernicus), to discover skills in medicine, or to ferret out the secret of the atom. God has other ways of letting us in on telephones, penicillin, and computers. But God has no book but the Bible to reveal himself as a God of infinite love. This is the Bible's purpose.

If we remember this, there will still be puzzling questions. How could God destroy the earth in Noah's flood? How could he approve or even order the genocide of whole peoples to protect the Israelites? How could he allow a good man, Job, to be the victim of one unjust tragedy after another?

If you are to find comfort in the Bible, you'll have to put these questions on the shelf and turn to the dominant motifs of the book. Don't start with Genesis, but with the Gospels. Go first to God the Son, who in his love for humanity gave his life on a cross for us. This may puzzle you even more. How can God love you that much?

But this is a comforting mystery, one that captures you for a life of meaning and mercy. With your eye on Jesus, you learn of God as a great and good father who hears the prayers of his children, guards them from evil, forgives their sins, and has a heavenly home prepared for them when death is done with them.

A God who punishes may be less puzzling than a God who forgives. All human beings know they deserve punishment. This is the way of simple justice. But to be caught up in a mercy that sweeps all our wretchedness away, to be received as if we had never sinned—can this be true?

This is the puzzle to end all puzzles. It is the truth to tower above all truths. It is the comfort to dwarf all other comforts.

Let the word of Christ dwell in you richly as you teach and admonish one another with all wisdom, and as you sing psalms, hymns, and spiritual songs with gratitude in your hearts to God.

   Colossians 3:16

5

When You're Troubled about Miracles

Did Jesus actually walk on the Sea of Galilee? Did he change water into wine at Cana? Did he instantly heal the ten lepers? Did he raise Lazarus from the dead?

These questions may trouble us in a scientific age. We've discovered the amazing orderliness of the universe, and it offends our reason to think that the God who gave us this gift of order would violate the gift. Some mischievous spirit perhaps, but God, oh no!

Most people who even bother to be troubled about miracles are willing to believe that God created the universe and that the man Jesus of Nazareth is God the Son come to earth. In a sense, they believe the two gigantic miracles (creation and incarnation) and are disturbed by the trivial ones.

How do we define a miracle? Something extraordinary for which there seems to be no scientific or rational explanation, like a person recovering from cancer when the doctors had given up? Or anything that baffles the imagination?

If my great-grandmother should return to earth for a week, her head would be swimming with the extraordinary—the miracles of the telephone, automobile, airplane, television, penicillin. These have become commonplace for us. If in wonder she should exclaim, "What has God done!" we might be startled out of our complacency to echo her question, "Yes, indeed, what amazing things hasn't God done with the knowledge he has given us?" After all, who put all these things in the universe, and who gave us probing minds to ferret them out? Are they any less miraculous or even mysterious because we find ways to explain them?

We are impoverished and dull if we fail to stand in wonder and awe at the staggering mystery of the ordinary. The daily conversation you have with a friend should send your little mind into orbit. Your brain sends impulses to the complicated machinery of your tongue and lips and diaphragm, and it produces sound waves. These waves strike your friend's eardrum and are translated into sound he hears, which in turn is transmitted to his brain as idea and meaning. If you're looking for something baffling, you need look no further.

Are biblical miracles so different? George Macdonald makes a delightful observation about Jesus changing water into wine at the wedding in Cana. He reminds us that every year God takes the seed of the grape and soil and sunshine and water (and a few weeks of time) and changes the water into wine—so why can't God compress the process into a moment of time? Why can't God have the ordinary become the extraordinary without annulling the orderliness of the universe and leaving us in chaos?

Even with the enormous explosion of knowledge in the last two centuries, the vast unknown (and perhaps unknowable) remains, giving us enough humility not to try to read the mind of God.

If you rest back in faith to believe that God created the universe—and you—and that Jesus of Nazareth is God come to earth to save us, then put the question of biblical miracles on the back shelf. Don't let these little, disturbing sideshows rob you of the big tent.

28

"Blessed are those who have not seen and yet have believed."
John 20:29

6

When You Question Your Spiritual Growth

All through nature we see growth. Plants grow and children grow. Astronomers say the universe itself is growing.

People who take the Christian faith seriously like some assurance that across the years they have grown in faith and hope and love.

Growth in the Spirit is not always easy to measure. In fact, spirituality itself is difficult to define. Is it an ecstasy of feeling? Is it essentially a moral quality? Is it awareness of God's presence?

Also, if you are growing spiritually, do you know it? Do others? And if you do grow, do you move on gradually or in spurts?

I have lived more than seventy years. Am I farther along now in my life with God (in my spirituality) than when I was eight or twelve? Do I have a greater childlike trust in God now than I did sixty years ago?

I have never felt a more sublime faith than the night my father was hovering between life and death in the next bedroom. I was thirteen, the oldest of six children. Full of fear, I crept into bed with mother and asked her what we would do if father were to die. I still remember her stroking my forehead saying, "God will take care of us." I fell asleep cradled in a great love and care. I don't think I have ever quite reached that point since.

Do I have a more selfless spirit? I'm not sure. Certainly at thirteen I never bothered to protect myself against the uncertainties of the future. It could be that now, with a few aches and pains that age brings on, I turn in on myself more than I did then.

Is my commitment to God stronger? I remember a striking moment in my senior year at college. It was spring and the sun was bright. I was sitting alone on the lawn in front of Old Main. Word had just come to me that I would be giving the valedictory for the class. Suddenly a sense of joy and gratitude swept through me. God had been enormously good to let me finish college, and I owed my life to him. That moment of commitment has never again come in quite that way. Was this the high moment of growth for me? Have I been on a plateau, or have I been slipping, ever since?

How about my level of hope? That ought to be one measure. I rather suspect that this has been eroding across the years. It's harder for me to hope now than when I was twenty or thirty. I'm not talking about hope in life after death, but about hope for life on earth for my grandchildren. I have fears I never had forty years ago.

The Scriptures do speak of our going from strength to strength. They speak of "mounting up on wings as eagles," of being renewed in the image of God, of growing more and more Christ-like. Growth should be our aim and hope.

But at best, to try to measure how we're doing has difficulties. It is easy for a person who has overcome drugs and alcoholism to chalk this up as gain, or for a person who was indifferent to church and worship who now hungers for the Word and for fellowship, or for a person who has overcome a passion for security and has begun to freely give money for the welfare of others. These gains are measurable, but the inner growth of the Spirit is not that easy to chart.

If God should grade us like a teacher to determine when we would qualify for his kingdom, where would we

31

be? When would we have peace? God knows the path of our progress, surely, our regress. But what does he do about it?

In one sense, God does nothing. We are God's, accepted simply because he created us and redeemed us to be his. We may reject God, but God never rejects us, whether we grow or slip.

The sacrament of Holy Baptism is just this kind of assurance. We became God's then, as spiritual babes. We became ones of his family, heirs of his kingdom. We've been living in that baptism ever since.

I know of nothing in all Scripture to compare with this towering truth to give us comfort. I don't have to feed my life into a computer to discover how I stand with Him.

Of course, I hope that these seventy years have not been barren, that the years have not brought regression. But I leave the measuring to him. If I have grown these sixty to seventy years, fine. I hope I have. If I've been slipping—God claims me still!

Now to him who is able to do immeasurably more than all we ask or imagine, according to his power that is at work within us, to him be the glory in the church and in Christ Jesus throughout all generations, for ever and ever! Amen.
Ephesians 3:20–21

7

When Your Church Fails You

If you're unhappy with your church, you'll find little comfort in shopping around for a church that will never fail you. And you'll find no comfort at all in giving up on all churches. You can hardly expect to keep your flame of faith glowing if you go it alone, drawing no warmth from others.

Churches do fail. For one reason or another, most congregations have an occasional bleak stretch. But unless the gospel itself has been lost, a dry period in the life of a church may set the stage for a fresh burst of the Spirit. It would be a pity to abandon the journey just as the road leads over the crest of the hill to new and exciting vistas.

The church of Jesus Christ, with its many denominations, has a vast variety of forms and styles of worship and living. It's quite right for you to find the one that best fits your temperament and taste. Some are stately and subdued, some are cozy and zealous, some are even rollicking and boisterous. Within their diversity, all may be faithful to their Lord. Your friend may like the meditative kind, you the jubilant kind. Most churches have variety within their own histories, but differences persist.

If your church is going through a cheerless period, or if present conditions prevent you from being edified, ask yourself some hard questions. Could it be that your discontent is more with yourself than with the church? The axiom, "You get out of it what you put into it," may be too simple an explanation for your uneasiness. But it is true that one person's faithfulness and enthusiasm can be come a contagion. It's amazing how a whole group can turn from lethargy and discouragement and come alive because of one person who spreads cheer and hope.

Sometimes the block is interpersonal relations. A wall has risen between you and the pastor, or between you and other members. A simple act of kindness could bring you together.

Maybe the pastor does not measure up to your expectations. Could it be that you had become overly attached to some former pastor and you have an emotional problem adjusting to the ways of the new one? Most pastors try earnestly to use the abilities God has given them. Your pastors may have fears and anxieties which they are bravely trying to hide from you. They may need you more than you need them.

Why do we belong to a church—to get something? We belong as an act of thanksgiving to God. At the hour of worship we come to give thanks, not primarily to receive. Of course we expect and need to receive comfort, correction, inspiration, instruction, hope. We are to open our hearts to receive what God may want to give us. Our moods, capricious and often unmanageable, may keep us from receiving what he wants to give. But we can thank God, whatever our moods. And we thank God best by asking God what he may want us to do. In doing for God, we open doors to his comfort.

"What's in it for me?" is a shabby basis for choosing a church or anything else. Selfishness is always counterproductive. It puts us on a dead-end street. Joy and contentment lie in a different direction.

And after all, what is your church? It does not belong to the pastor or to the boards or to the choirs. The church belongs to Christ, and you belong to him. In a strange sense, you yourself are the church, at least as much as any other person in the congregation. Don't ever say it's "Pastor Smith's church" or "their church" or even "the church." Say "my church."

You may have every right to say, "My church has become a dull place. It's lost some of the zeal it once had, and I have a hard time feeling the joy I should have." But the spirit of God lurks in your church. God waits to fan your languishing spirits into new and joyous life. And the key to just that kind of renewal may lie in your hands.

> *You are no longer foreigners and aliens, but fellow citizens with God's people and members of God's household, built on the foundation of the apostles and prophets, with Christ Jesus himself as the chief cornerstone.*
> *Ephesians 2:19–20*

For Further Reading

The Color of the Night: Reflections on Suffering and the Book of Job
Gerhard E. Frost

Jesus, Remember Me: Words of Assurance from Martin Luther
edited by Barbara Owen

All Will Be Well: A Gathering of Healing Prayers
edited by Lyn Klug

Wrestling with Depression: A Spiritual Guide to Reclaiming Life
William and Lucy Hulme

Journey of the Heart: Reflections on Life's Way
Gerhard E. Frost

Liferails: Holding Fast to God's Promises
Scott Walker

Our Hope for Years to Come: The Search for Spiritual Sanctuary
Reflections and Photographs
Martin Marty and Micah Marty

Diary of an Old Soul
George MacDonald